ALAN RANGER

2 cm Flak 28 & 30

Published in Poland in 2022
by Wydawnictwo Stratus sp.j.
Żeromskiego 4,
27-600 Sandomierz, Poland
e-mail: office@wydawnictwostratus.pl

as
MMPBooks
e-mail: office@mmpbooks.biz

www.mmpbooks.biz
www.wydawnictwostratus.pl

ISBN
978-83-66549-10-4

Editor in chief
Roger Wallsgrove

Editorial Team
Bartłomiej Belcarz
Robert Pęczkowski
Artur Juszczak
Dr Chris Lloyd-Staples

Cover concept
Dariusz Grzywacz

Book layout concept
Dariusz Grzywacz

All photos: author's collection except stated

DTP
Wydawnictwo Stratus sp.j.

PRINTED IN POLAND

Foreword

In this series of books, I have no intention of trying to add to what is already a very well documented history of Germany's anti-aircraft weapons systems, their crews and associated equipment as it has been thoroughly covered by previous publications. Here I hope to give an impression through original photographs, taken both during and before war, of both the 2 cm Flak 28 and Flak 30 and their crews in all the various theatres of operation they found themselves operating in. Here in this publication I hope to show what was seen through the lens of the normal German soldier's camera; the soldiers that had to live with and operate these weapons each and every day, not the professional PK cameramen whose well posed and sanitized shots are well known and have been published over and over again. As such they have been seen by most interested parties by now already, however the images taken by individual soldiers show a more personal view of the weapon systems and their installations that the soldiers both lived and worked on, the views that interested the common soldier not the professional propagandist. For the most part these photographs have been in private collections and have only recently come onto the market. Most images we have used here were taken from prints made on old German Agfa paper stock and the majority of these original prints are no more than 25 mm by 45 mm in size. Whilst we have used the best quality photos from my collection, occasionally due to the interesting or the rare nature of the subject matter a photo of a lesser quality has been included.

2 cm Flak 28

The origin of this legendary weapon was a gun designed in 1914 by Reinhold Becker, first used on a few of Germany's larger aircraft towards the end of World War One. After the First World War Germany was prohibited from possessing anti-aircraft guns, by the restrictions placed on Germany by the victorious allies in article 169 of the Treaty of Versailles. In 1919 Reinhold Becker sold the rights to his design to the Swiss company of Semag, and Semag was in turn bought out by Werkzeug- und Maschinenfabrik Oerlikon in the early 1920s.

Werkzeug- und Maschinenfabrik Oerlikon, more commonly known as just Oerlikon, sold both production licenses and actual weapons to many of Europe's governments and arms manufacturers in the 1920s and early 1930s, including manufacturers in England, Belgium and France, all of whom produced variations of weapons based on the basic Oerlikon design. However, despite Germany's signing of the Treaty of Versailles, as soon as the Allied Military Control Commission ceased operations in Germany in 1926, Rheinmetall began secretly to set up manufacture of a version of the Oerlikon 2 cm weapon in one of their subsidiary companies based in Switzerland. Deliveries started in 1928. Germany from 1926 also purchased 2 cm Oerlikon weapons from other foreign-based producers via a chain of shell companies. These weapons, along with the Rheinmetall-Borsig production weapons, were introduced into the German armed forces as the 2 cm Flak 28.

The 2 cm Flak 28 was a gas-operated magazine-fed weapon. To fire the gun, it had first to be cocked; this was done by pulling back the breech manually, compressing the recoil spring and setting the firing hammer back from the firing pin within the beech block. Once the gun was fully cocked the recoil spring would force the breech block back towards the barrel, and during the breech block's travel back to the firing position it would pick up a round from the box magazine that held 15 rounds and place it in the firing chamber of the barrel. After pressing the trigger, that was hand operated and located under the breech block, the hammer would hit the firing pin in the breech block which would hit the percussion cap in the base of the cartridge and fire the round. The breech block would now be forced backwards by the gas pressure, ejecting the empty cartridge case and also recocking the firing hammer and compressing the recoil spring. If the trigger was pulled again the firing process would be repeated.

The weapon could be used on wheels with its special tripod legs (*Spreizlafette*) locked up, the two rear legs folded together and hinged under the centre of the gun cradle. The front leg was detached and stowed on top of the two folded together rear legs. These legs now formed the gun's trail and the hitching point for any towing vehicle. In this configuration the trail and the two wheels formed a tripod base. The Flak 28 could also fire on its *Spreizlafette* carriage, the gun cradle's base plate that the legs attached to. The wheels were removed, the front leg was locked in place under the base plate pointing forward, and the two back legs were separated and locked into position forming a tripod base. In difficult terrain, the weapon could be disassembled and transported by pack animals in three loads, the barrel and recoil system in one, gun cradle and its base plate in the second and the wheels with the tripod legs forming the third.

A gun crew of four was required to operate the weapon. The gunner fired the gun via a trigger on the breech in the semi-automatic role, but by using a lever to the right of the trigger the gun could be fired in the fully automatic role via a foot operated trigger. The weapon was aimed by using one of the interchangeable mounted gun sights. For ground targets the gun was fitted with a ring and bead set of sights, however from the beginning of WWII for aerial engagements the Flak 28s were issued with the Linealvisier 21. This was a mechanical programmable optical unit. One member of the gun crew had to adjust the optics via turn knobs that moved graduated lenses within the optic to values called out by another member of the crew, who would be using a stereoscopic range finder, usually either the type EM34 or the EM36 *Entfernungsmesser*. Finally, the fourth crew member would be responsible for loading the weapon.

Since both the effectiveness of the projectile and the ballistic properties of the Flak 28 were roughly the same as that of the Flak 30 and 38, the Flak 28 was used until the war's end, mostly in homeland defence roles, but many were also used on the Atlantic wall defences and as airfield protection in the occupied areas. The 2 cm bore of the weapon was the same as the Flak 30/38 and the same projectiles could be fitted into the propellant-filled cartridge case. However due to differences in the dimensions of the Flak 28's 2 cm shell propellant cartridge cases, it was unable to use the same 2 cm rounds as the German 2 cm Flak 30/38. In order to secure a reliable supply of ammunition Germany built their own production facilities to produce rounds for the Flak 28 from 1936 onwards. The Flak 28 cartridge case was slightly shorter and had a larger circumference than the Flak 30/38 cartridge cases.

Germany purchased and manufactured a number of these weapons before the war, however stocks of the Flak 28 increased exponentially following the victory in France and the Low Countries as many of the now occupied nations had purchased large numbers of the same Oerlikon, or similar weapons, from Switzerland directly in the 1930s. These were now all absorbed into the German arsenal and as such the 2 cm Flak 28s, as they were all designated, became a common weapon within the German armed forces. However, in common with the Flak 30, by 1939 its rate of fire was not considered adequate and as such it was for the most part relegated to use in the aforementioned second line defensive role, mostly in static point defence.

Technical Data:
Weight 483kgs
Gun Crew of 4
Elevation -12 to +90°
Traverse 360°
Round Weight 300 Grams
Muzzle Velocity 830 m/sec
Maximum Range 4,400 m
Maximum Effective Height 3,700 m.
Practical Rate of Fire 100 to 120 rounds per minute

2 cm Flak 30

The German company Rheinmetall developed the gas-operated 2 cm Flak 30, named after the year in which the design was approved. The weapon however actually entered service with the German armed forces in 1934 and was an improved version of Rheinmetall-Borsig's earlier weapon that had been designed for the German Navy (Kriegsmarine), the 2 cm MG C/30 L, that itself was a development of the Solothurn ST-5. The Flak 30 was not only produced by Rheinmetall-Borsig, Ostmark Werke GmbH / Werk Gbell near Prague (Praha-Kbely) in the Reich Protectorate of Czechoslovakia also participated in its manufacture.

The weapon could be equipped with one of two different flash eliminators that screwed onto the end of the barrel. When the weapon was new it was fitted with a flash eliminator that had an inner diameter of 35mm, whilst when worn in it was retrofitted with a flash eliminator that had an inner diameter of 41 mm, which affected the recoil less and also increased the rate of fire. The theoretical rate of fire was 280 rounds per minute, but the practically achievable rate of fire was only 120 rounds per minute.

The weapon was operated by a crew of five. The actual gunner (K1) both fired and aimed the weapon whilst on a seat fixed to the centre line of the gun cradle and could fire the gun in either the automatic or semi-automatic modes by the use of foot operated pedal triggers. The pedal on the right of the gun's cradle was for semi-automatic fire and the pedal on the left for fully automatic. It was aimed using one of the interchangeable sights – for aerial targets the Flak 30 was initially equipped with the same *Linealvisier* 21 optical sights as the Flak 28 but this sight was eventually replaced by the improved *Flakvisier* 35 that was phased into the weapon's production. For engaging ground targets, the weapon came equipped with a standard direct vision 3x8 telescopic sight. Another crewman (K2), when the *Linealvisier* 21 was attached, had to adjust the optics via turn knobs that moved graduated lenses within the optic to values called out by the third crew member (K3), who would use a stereoscopic range finder, either the *Entfernungsmesser* type EM34 or the EM36. The fourth and fifth crew members (K4&K5) would be responsible for loading the weapon. An experienced crew would often dispense with the Linealvisier 21 gun sight and use the standard telescopic sights against aerial targets as well, because the *Linealvisier* 21 had been found wanting when newer faster allied aircraft were encountered.

The weapon was loaded from the left-hand side and fed from a 20-round capacity curved box type magazine. The Flak 30 had an overall weight of 463 kg when fitted with a 1.3 metre barrel. It could be traversed the full 360° and could be elevated through -12° to +90°. The gun cradle was mounted onto a triangular base/frame that had an adjustable foot at each corner, to allow for levelling the gun platform. This base/frame was designed to be able to be picked up by and transported with the standard German trailer unit, type Sd. Ah. 51.

The Flak 30 could be fitted with a gun shield that weighed 112 kg, which was supposed to only be fitted when the gun was expected to encounter ground targets. But in service this shield was usually left in place and can be seen to be in place on the vast majority of the existing photographs of the weapon in service.

The Flak 30 was eventually issued to the German Navy and designated the CL/38. It was also sold to China, but perhaps more interestingly to the Dutch army. Most of these weapons I imagine were soon back in German hands come the summer of 1940.

Whilst in general the Flak 30 can be considered a success, it did suffer from a an annoying jamming issue that was never fully resolved and this, along with the need to increase the rate of fire to combat the ever-faster enemy aircraft, led to the Flak 30 being superseded by the Flak 38. Although the gun was never withdrawn from service it was no longer considered a front-line weapon and wherever possible commanders replaced it with newer weapons.

Of note is that German company of Mauser was contracted to design and produce a lighter more portable version of the Flak 30, for issue to Germany's mountain and airborne parachute divisions. This resulted in the much lighter "2 cm Geb-FlaK 38"(*Gebirgsflugabwehrkanone* 38), that entered service in early 1942. The weapon was basically the same, the redesign mostly affecting the gun cradle and operating systems (elevation and traversing gears) by making use of steel stampings rather than heavier cast components. It also eliminated the triangular base/frame completely, replacing it with a much lighter tripod base similar to that originally found on the Flak 28.

Whist the most common anti-aircraft round to be fired from this weapon was the high explosive incendiary blast grenade, that had a range of 4,800 meters and an effective vertical range of 3,700 metres with a muzzle velocity of 900 metres per second, many other types of 2 cm rounds were available.

Technical Data;
Weight 463 kgs
Gun Crew of 5
Elevation -12 to +90°
Traverse 360°
Muzzle Velocity 900 m/sec
Maximum Range 4,800 m
Maximum Effective Height 3,700 m
Practical Rate of Fire 120 rounds per minute

The German 2 cm Flak 30 & Flak 38 Ammunition

A wide variety of 20x138B ammunition was manufactured to be used by both the 2 cm Flak 30 and 38 weapons. Some of the more commonly used types are listed in the table below. Other ammo types in existence included numerous practice rounds (marked *Übung* or *Üb*, using the German the abbreviation) and a number of different armour-piercing types. A high-velocity PzGr 40 round with a tungsten carbide core in an aluminium body also existed in the 20x138B calibre.

German Designation	Projectiles weight in grams	Projectiles Explosive charge	Description
Sprenggranatpatrone L'spur mit Zerleger	115 g	6.0 g High Explosive (Pentaerythritol Tetranitrate)	Nose tip fused tracer round, self-destruct at 5.5 seconds (2000m range) due to tracer burn-through.
Sprenggranatpatrone L'spur mit Zerleger	120 g	6.6 g High Explosive (Pentaerythritol Tetranitrate)	Boat-tailed HE tracer round with nose fuse. Self-destruct at approximately 2 km range due to tracer burn-through.
Brandsprenggranatpatrone L'spur mit Zerleger	120 g	2.4 g High Explosive (Cyclotrimethylenetrinitramine & Wax) known as RDX (Research Department eXplosive) as well as 4.1g of Incendiary (Zinc)	Nose tip fuse, tracer (5 second burn), with self-destruct due to tracer burn-through.
Brandsprenggranatpatrone mit Zerleger	120 g	22 g total (High Explosive and Incendiary)	Nose tip fuse, no tracer, with self-destruct, lack of tracer and high density of phosphorous incendiary allowed more filling load.
Panzergranatpatrone L'spur mit Zerleger	146 g	no surviving recorded specification	Base-fused tracer round, with self-destruct due to tracer burn-through after 2 second flight (approximately 1000m range).
Panzerbrandgranatpatrone (Phosphor) L'spur ohne Zerleger	148 g	3.0 g Incendiary (White Phosphorous)	Tracer round, with no fuse or self-destruct functions.
Panzersprenggranatpatrone L'spur mit Zerleger (Kriegsmarine)	121 g	3.6 g High Explosive	Base-fused round, self-destruct after 4.5 second flight (approximately 1800m range) due to tracer burn-through.

2 cm Flak 28

A 2 cm Flak 28 set up in a temporary firing position protected by a surrounding wall made up of stacked pieces of turf. The weapon is providing cover for a temporary advanced air strip somewhere in eastern France during the invasion of 1940. The photograph was taken on the 6th June that year. Clearly shown is the Flak 28's distinctive vertically-mounted 20 round capacity magazine with its permanently fixed exterior carrying handle.

Above: Seen here in a semi-permanent firing pit, again surrounded by cut pieces of turf, on the perimeter of a captured and re-tasked Dutch military airfield, a Flak 28 at the ready. At this point of the campaign in the west a permanent watch would have been established over all the advanced airfields used in the campaign and no doubt this weapon was just one of many of a variety of types set to provide protection against possible retaliatory air attack. This photo was taken on 19th of May 1940 at Fliegerhors airfield in the west of Holland, 4 km WNW of Alkmaar and 2.5 km south of Bergen. It later became a permanent fighter base used by both *Luftwaffe* day and night fighter squadrons.

Right: This photograph was taken by the same soldier as the picture above but sometime prior to the first one, as *Fliegerhors* airfield was only taken over by the *Luftwaffe* on the 16th of May. Taken not long before the picture above, but here we see a Flak 28 set up within the airfield perimeter in a fully exposed position. I am sure it did not stay that way for long. Of interest to me is the relaxed nature of the crew, bearing in mind the front line could not have been that far off at this time although the allies were in full retreat.

A great photograph taken during a firing drill, readiness training session by a flak unit equipped with the Flak 28 guarding Dortmund rail yards in August 1940. Of note here are the uniforms of the crew, two wearing drill training uniforms and the other two seen here wearing all white fatigues. They are setting the sighting mechanism. The guns quick change barrel locking nut/ferrule can be clearly seen at the base of the barrel and also the front of the gun's mounting cradle. The ring of the ring and bead mechanical sighting system with its windage indicator can also be seen. Lastly, in the very background one of the detachable transport wheels with its stub axle is to be found on the ground behind the gunner's head. It is of the late type fitted with a pneumatic tyre.

Here we have a 20 mm Oerlikon Gun (identical to a Flak 28) in full transport mode with its sights and magazine removed and its tripod support legs configured to become its towing bar. One leg was rigidly fixed to the guns base plate whilst the other two legs could be unlocked and pivoted around to fix to the rigid leg, albeit just below it and they when locked in that position also formed the towing ring hitching point. The gun barrel has been rotated so that it aligns with the rigid leg such that the barrel is protected from damage, safe above folded legs that now make up the towing bar. This is an early weapon - its wheels are fitted with solid vulcanized rubber tyres. Note the horse-drawn wagon that it is being towed by; this gun was captured in the first days of the invasion of the west from the Belgian military and has been pressed into service by a horse-drawn supply unit. The only location information I have was written on the reverse of the picture and states the photo was taken during the summer of 1940 in Flanders.

A group of this flak unit's officers are pictured here playing (familiarising themselves) with one of their unit's Flak 28s located on top of a wooden flak tower in the spring of 1942, somewhere around industrial side of the city of Osnabruck, Germany. This photo give us a good view of the gun mount and its folding tripod legs.

This Flak 28 is located in a brick revetment on the perimeter of an airfield in the suburbs of Amiens, France and belongs to Light Flak Regiment 680 (le.Flak Abt. 680), seen here in the summer of 1943. A good view is provided of the cast lattice reinforced side of the gun cradle

Left: Here we have another Flak 28 in its gun pit on the channel coast of France in the autumn of 1941. Seen here are the weapon's gunnery control wheels, and seen is the mounting base of the gunner's seat and one of his foot rests.

Top left photo: Located on a Flak platform mounted on top of a factory roof in the town of Hengelo, Holland, this undated photo of a Flak 28 offers us a good view of the left hand side of the weapon. We can see the gunner's traversing hand wheel and the other side of the gunner's seat mount, as well a clear view of the left side of the gun cradle.

Top right photo: Photographed on the 21st of September 1938 this Flak 28 is seen on a firing range located close to the Baltic coast of northern Germany. It shows to good effect the gunner's position and should be of good use when (hopefully!) a kit is issued for this beautifully engineered and, to me at least, good looking weapon.

Bottom photo: A posed photograph of a Flak 28 in its wood lined gun pit. The soldier is one Heinrich Schmidt who is proudly showing off his newly awarded Iron Cross 2nd class, earned by being credited with the shooting down of a British light bomber. Given the date of September 1940 the bomber in question was most likely a Fairey Battle or a Bristol Blenheim. The action in question may have taken place earlier in the year during the invasion of France. This view gives us a good look at the gunner's seat in its firing position – the seat folded up when in the weapon's travelling configuration

Left: This interesting photograph of a Flak 28 was taken on June 24th 1940 in a repurposed French coastal installation. The mounts for the coastal defence artillery sighting optics that were previously positioned here are still clearly visible protruding from the concrete floor. Battle damage is still very much in evidence on the side walls of the protective pit.

Bottom: A most curious photo this one, not for the Flak 28 set up in the foreground or even the artillery piece limber in the background. It is purported by the inscriptions on its rear to have been taken by a German naval unit on the Spanish Island of El Hierro Santa Cruz off Tenerife, part of the Spanish-owned Canary Islands off the west coast of Africa in 1940. Whilst I am aware that Germany navy units often used the Canary Islands as a port of call and had a very good rela-tion-ship with the islands, I was not aware that they ever put troops ashore other than for shore leave R&R purposes. This photo, if it is to be believed, throws this into doubt.

Above: A candid view of a Flak 28 and its crew in a relaxed mode. No doubt this informal pose was struck without an officer in sight, as to be seen consuming a bottle of wine whilst on duty is frowned upon in all the worlds' military of any time period. I particularly like the cocked helmet on the soldier using the field telephone. The photo was taken on 15th July 1942 somewhere in northern Holland.

Below: This melancholy photo shows a look-out manning his post during the summer of 1942 in a gun pit located on the coast of the Channel Island of Jersey. The Channel Islands were the only part of Britain that would ever be under German occupation. Of interest here is the white painted code on the 20 round magazine. Units often had a symbol-based system to use as a quick way to identify the magazine's load (type of round selection loaded into it). Rounds were usually mixed – as an example every fifth round being a tracer and may be the last three rounds also – so the gun crew knew to change the magazine without having to count the number of rounds being shot.

This Flak 28 is set up in a very exposed location, probably on a range or training ground as it is a most unlikely location to set up a firing position in a war zone. It was taken in August 1941 but I have no more information than that. It does however show the Flak 28 in an unobscured way, offering us a good overall view of the weapon. Also note one of the transport wheels and stub axles in the rear, it looks to be of the type fitted with solid non-pneumatic tyres.

Bottom: Photographed on a firing range that was part of the Luneburg Heath training grounds in northern Germany, this is the gun section of the 2nd Platoon of Light Flak Regiment 680. Of note is the gunnery observation tower in the background and the single officer standing to the rear of the gun section. The photo was taken in August 1939, just prior to war being declared by Britain and France on the 3rd of September of the same year.

Another informal group photo, this time taken in barracks at Hamburg, Germany on the 4th May 1939. This picture gives us a good view of the right front of the Flak 28. Note the wide apart setting for the gunner's foot rests, I doubt the gunner was seated in much comfort after any length of time. Also in focus is the forward part of the ring and bead gun sight. Note it is offset from the centre line and attached directly to the gun's barrel. It can only have been used as rough indication of the ' location as it would move with the barrel in recoil and wobble about considerably when the gun was being fired. No doubt the gunner used the projectiles' tracers to follow the arc of fire once a target had been engaged.

This is a great view of a gun that is part of an airfield's mobile anti-aircraft defence. Many of the coastal airfields employed a mobile Flak unit as part of the airfield's protection, so any reconnaissance photos taken by the enemy could never for certain show all the flak sites around any target, making planning a strafing run a dangerous mission to undertake. Of interest here is the great view of the gun overall and the crew's personal weapons (Mauser rifle/Karabiner 98Ks) as well as an EM34 or EM36 *Entfernungsmesser* 1 meter binocular rangefinder stood up against a pile of 2 cm magazines in the background.

Here we see a Flak 28 set up in a recently harvested wheat field with a hay bale bund built up around it. The gun has been positioned there as protection for the railway that is just hidden from view, due to it being lower than the surrounding ground whilst running through a revetment. However the tell-tail telegraph poles bear witness to it location. Note the crew's personal weapons lying on the top of the hay bales in the back ground and the camouflaged poncho in the foreground, probably laid out to dry after being used as part of a tent the night before.

A great informal portrait of this Flak 28 gun's crew, taken from the steps that lead up to this roof top flak tower. Many such wooden constructions were erected in the first part of the war, as the war progressed many were replaced by concrete flak towers or other more permanent types of structures. The crew are from a *Luftwaffe* division as indicated by the *Luftwaffe* eagle seen on the helmet in the foreground.

Mounted on top of a brand new timber Flak tower constructed just north of Aachen, Germany we can see a Flak that has just been set up and has yet to be tied down (the crew will fix the gun to the wood deck to prevent it being moved around by the recoil forces of the gun) most common in this type of installation wooden chocks would be placed by each of the three leg ends and they would be nailed to the deck. Of note here is the metal hand rail above the hatch way in the floor one of the sides of the two part hatch is open whist the other is closed. The small round object seen hanging from the bottom of the gun's tripod base is the screw on cover that when in place would protect the glass cover of the gun base's built in spirit level.

The crew of this Flak 28 are pictured in a relaxed pose around their charge whilst one of the crew paints on a new kill mark in the form of a white ring around the barrel. The photo was taken close to the village of Altenwalde on coast the North sea in the area of the Heligoland Bight. The photo was taken on the 1st of June 1940 during the battle of Dunkirk and it was probably an RAF aircraft trying to prevent German Naval shipping getting involved in the evacuation that fell prey to this gun. The gun was positioned at a point that enabled it to protect the ports of Wilhelmshaven, Bremerhaven and Hamburg.

A Flak 28 in a timber-lined gun pit on the perimeter of Leeuwarden airfield that is located 4 km North-West of Leeuwarden town, Holland. This Dutch airfield was vastly developed by the occupying German *Luftwaffe* throughout the war. Of note is the goal post of a football pitch that has been established on the perimeter of the base, and lastly a clear view gunner's seated position which does not look as if it could have been comfortable to be in for any length of time.

This Flak 28 is situated in its wooed-lined gun pit on the channel coast dug into the cliffs above the port of Boulogne-Sur-Mer in the late summer of 1940. By 1943 most of Atlantic Wall construction was well under way in this part of the French coast and no doubt this position was replaced by a concrete gun emplacement, many hundreds of which are still to be found in the area to this day.

2 cm Flak 30

This photo of a Flak 30 gives us a good full view of the weapon; it is atop a wooden flak tower built on the roof of one of the Siemens Factory buildings in Neuhaus, Germany. The photo was taken on 7th November 1942

Both the photographs on this page were taken on the 13th of July 1942 in a concrete gun position on the coast of France just north of Le Havre. Of note here is the unobstructed view they provide of the front of the weapon without a gun shield fitted. In the upper photo we can clearly see the foot operated trigger pedals above the heel rests that are mounted directly to the rotating gun platform base. Also of interest are the quick reference guides located on the gun pit wall – we can see the 9 o'clock marker behind the gunner. The use of clock positions around the walls of the gun pit enabled the gunner to easily follow target information given by the battery commander. We can also see one of what would have been many horizon silhouettes that have predetermined range information marked on them. These would enable the gunner to know the range of a target as it flew close to one of the features marked up on the silhouette.

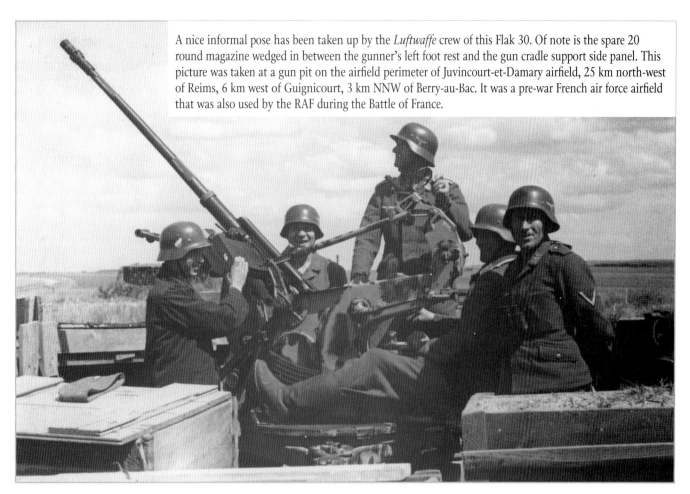

A nice informal pose has been taken up by the *Luftwaffe* crew of this Flak 30. Of note is the spare 20 round magazine wedged in between the gunner's left foot rest and the gun cradle support side panel. This picture was taken at a gun pit on the airfield perimeter of Juvincourt-et-Damary airfield, 25 km north-west of Reims, 6 km west of Guignicourt, 3 km NNW of Berry-au-Bac. It was a pre-war French air force airfield that was also used by the RAF during the Battle of France.

Below: This Flak 30 is situated along the Pas de Calais, France. It was photographed in June 1941. The gun pit was later made into a concrete emplacement as part of the Atlantic Wall, but in the summer of 1941 it was still just a log and turf filled wall protected gun site. Of note here are the concrete cinder blocks the gun's three mounting pads are placed on and the raised timber floor fitted around the gun's base plate; no doubt it proved necessary in the winter of 1940/41. Also of interest is the tin box by the side of the gun, the storage tin for the gun's cleaning tools.

A good photograph of a Flak 30 pictured on the Luneburg training grounds in northern Germany. This view shows to good advantage the position the gunner would be in if the unit were engaging a ground target. However in this instance the gunner is actually a senior officer just having a look through the sights and playing at being a gunner, in the guise of again familiarising himself with the unit's equipment. Note the travel lock, that is in its unlocked raised position and seen under the gun's recoil cradle.

Here we have a Flak 30 undergoing maintenance. The barrel has been replaced with a factory-fresh brand new barrel and the crew are cleaning off the grease that was factory applied as a protective coating for it whilst in storage. The two crew doing the cleaning are using cotton rags to perform the task. The inside of the barrel would also require a very good clean, using both of the pull-through heads included in the cleaning kit – the wire brush and the leather pad.

Above: A Flak 30 emplaced in a field in the grounds of a factory in western Germany. Protection of the German industrial complexes became a much higher priority as the war went on and the abilities of the allied bomber force improved exponentially. When this photo was taken in September 1940 the only threat that this flak crew might have to face would be a lone squadron of Vickers Wellingtons or Armstrong Whitworth Whitleys, neither of which would have posed a huge threat to them or the factory they were guarding.

Below: An exposed position such as this on the Dutch West Frisian Islands would not have been much fun in winter, however the job had to be done. The gun's associated equipment stowage boxes lie all around. The tin box in the foreground with the stamped rib strengtheners I do not recognise but the long box behind it is a spare barrel box and the box immediately behind that is for the EM34 or EM36 *Entfernungsmesser* 1 meter binocular range finder, that can be seen being used by the crewman standing behind the Flak 30's gunner.

Above: Photographed during a training exercise around the Frankfurt area in late 1938, we see here a Flak 30 still attached to its towing trailer, the Sd. Ah. 51. It is being manhandled into its firing position by its crew. Of note is the barrel's muzzle brake cover and the gun's canvas cover. Whilst the muzzle brake cover is the factory issue, the gun's weather cover is a crew addition. The factory supplied tailored cover has no doubt been damaged or lost at some point, this was not uncommon as they were not particularly robust and in service are rarely to be seen after any length of time.

Below: "Life goes on" – a crew member is seen here sitting on the gunner's seat of this Flak 30 reading a newspaper. Surprisingly this photograph was taken in late June 1940 just after the occupation of Paris whilst fighting was still going on. One would not have been impressed by this crew's choice of location for the setting up of the firing position – on top of a berm is hardly a stable platform from which to fire. It is hard to believe that a better location could not have been found close to the narrow gauge railway seen in the background. This photo was taken in the Flers area of Normandy.

This atmospheric photograph was taken on the banks of the Gent-Brugge Canal in Belgium during May 1940, it offers us a good look at a Flak 30 fitted with an armoured shield. Note in the background, laid down on the towpath of the canal, is an EM34 or EM36 *Entfernung-smesser* range finder fitted to its shoulder frame that help the operator take its weight and hold it steady whilst taking a range reading.

This is more typical of the type of pose that soldiers informally took for a picture to send home. One *Luftwaffe* crew member points out an imaginary target and the other is pointing his P08 Luger side arm in the same general direction. One notable thing this photo does show us of the Flak 30 is the extent the three mounting pads can be used to level the gun base. The rear pad is not visible as it is wound to its highest point and the pad in the foreground is wound down to its full extent in order to level the gun platform.

Above: Taken during an exercise this photo shows us a Flak 30 mounted in its transport trailer the Sd. Ah. 51. The crew appear to be setting up the trailer's front stand, a folding tubular apparatus attached to the front of the trailer just behind the towing shackle. A peculiarity of the Sd. Ah. 51 is the tin box attached to its frame behind the mudguard that only held one 20 round magazine, whereas in all other flak trailers stowage boxes held a minimum of two magazines, as did the standard ammunition stowage box that 2 cm ammunition was supplied in.

Bottom: This Flak 30 is set up in a gun pit dug in to the bare earth and is located somewhere in Holland during the invasion in May 1940. The whole flak crew is seen posing for a photo to send home. Many items of interest here, among them is the soldier wearing the shoulder frame fitted to an EM34 or EM36 *Entfernungsmesser* range finder and the fact that many of the crew are wearing their pre-war GM24 gas mask in its canvas bag.

Seen in the grounds of a manor house in northern Holland in the autumn of 1942 that is being used as officers' quarters of a *Luftwaffe* unit, a Flak 30 is to be found sited in the open, set up on a wooden platform that is visibly bowed by the weight of the weapon. Of interest in this picture is the non-standard ready ammunition stowage box mounted to the side of the gun frame side panel. It looks to only be able to hold one magazine and probably was removed from an Sd. Ah. 51. Lastly we can see the gunner on lookout is wearing sunglasses, a rather rare item in the 1940s but an item that was often issued to Flak gunners and became a prized possession.

This gun crew pose with their 2 cm Flak 30 next to a taxiway of Frankfurt Am Main Airfield in July of 1939. Again note the sunglasses being worn by the gunner and also the plethora of standard 2 cm flak ammunition boxes in the foreground. Each box (tin) held two 20 round magazines fitted in opposing directions within the box which made them easier to get a hold of and take out quickly. Lastly of note in this picture is the huge contrast between the panzer grey gun cradle and its mounting base and the fitted 2 cm cannon that is oil blued and unpainted.

A great photograph of a Flak 30 in a hand dug gun pit. This detailed photo shows the *Flakvisier* 35 gun sight, its mounting, and the aiming point follower arms that kept it in line with the gun as a target was tracked. Also visible alongside the gun sight is the German version of a Picatinny Rail that the direct vision 3x8 telescopic sight was attached to for engaging ground targets. Lastly of note are the personal items of clothing that the crew are wearing instead of uniform. This was a common practice although rarely seen in official photographs and it does offer us a look into the real life of a flak crew in 1941 during the battle of France. Whilst the location was not recorded on this photo the date is stated as the 8th of June 1940.

Both the photos on this page are of the same Flak 30 and *Waffen-SS* gun crew. The photos were taken on the frosty morning of 23rd November 1944 somewhere on the Eastern Front. No location is given, but of interest is the very fact that this Flak 30 is still in front line use and that the gun has both its sights fitted. However, even at this late stage this gun, like most Flak 30s, did not have a gun shield fitted. Finally, note the camouflaged uniforms that the crew are wearing.

This photograph is an oddity. The same image was used in an official German forces post card, but the post card provides a much grainier low quality image than this photo. During the war, copies of many original photos were available for purchase by troops and this is probably one of them. Its shows a most unrealistic sight of a *Luftwaffe* crew in action, all wearing full dress uniform including white shirts with neck ties, bayonets with ceremonial knots, and Model 1916 helmets. The M33 marching boots have three straps on each side. Obviously a posed shot, but it does give us a nice detail view of the Flak 30 in profile.

A great photo of a Flak 30 from behind, showing us much of the detail of the sighting apparatus and mechanical details of the elevation and traversing mechanisms. The gunner's seat and the firing pedals are also clearly visible. The photo was taken in 1941 in a timber-built emplacement that is part of the defensive positions erected around a field engineered bridge across the River Bug in Russia.

This photo is another image that was used on an official German forces post card but also available for soldiers to purchase during the war. This service was devised as not all soldiers had access to a camera and yet still would have liked to have photo to keep or send home. This photo in my collection appears to be the same as many others printed on photographic paper with an image size of approx. 25mm by 45mm. The image is still of interest as it shows a Flak 30 being manhandled into its firing position whilst still attached to its Sd. Ah. 51 towing trailer unit. Clearly visible in the foreground are the two hooks that form part of the trailer's frame, slotted into the two lifting shackles mounted on the gun's base plate.

This photograph was taken atop a Flak tower on the outskirts of Duisburg, Germany. It is dated 25ᵗʰ September 1941. Later in the war the flak defence around Duisburg's Demag factory was much improved, with three large multi-storey concrete Flak towers, one of which still survives. It is currently being used as a training climbing wall for mountaineering classes, as well as an aerial installation for the local radio club.

On parade in the quadrangle of Frankfurt barracks, this photo shows a parade for Hitler's birthday on 20ᵗʰ April 1939. The Flak 30 on its Sd. Ah. 51 trailer in view is in immaculate condition and also painted in an early war camouflage scheme of Panzer Grey, Tan Brown and Dark Green. Of note is the age of the troops on the right of the photo. They can only be Hitler Youth I would have thought, but it is odd that they are in full army uniform with WW1 steel helmets. Maybe they are in a cadet corps??

Although this appears to be a private soldier's photo it is another of the postcard images that must have been purchased by the soldier who created the photo album that I purchased in the late 1990s. However of interest is that the unit has no field telephone or radio, and communication between the Flak gun here and the unit controller is achieved by signal paddles and a megaphone. Whilst it is not dated, it must have been taken after the mid-1930s as communication equipment such as a field telephone was basic equipment by 1937, and this is undoubtedly a training exercise.

This photo of a Flak 30 on the Adriatic coast was taken during the invasion of Yugoslavia (Führer Directive No. 25) in April of 1941. Other than the good view of the front of a Flak 30, it also at first glance appears to be odd because the gunner and the two soldiers in the far background are seen to be wearing gasmasks and the soldier wearing the range finder rig also has his gas mask out of its container and it can be seen hung on his waist belt. However according to the note on the photo's reverse they are using their gasmasks for protection from sand. As the wind often gusted on the coast it picked up fine sand and made vision awkward – wearing their gasmasks negated the issue and enabled them to see better.

This Flak 30 is in a well-constructed gun pit in northern Ukraine. Whilst the Flak 30 is as always the centre of attention, notable here is its lack of a fitted gun sight – neither its *Flakvisier* 35 or its direct vision 3x8 telescopic sight are seen to be fitted. I think the field craft deserves a mention here, note the log circle filled with compacted earth that forms the gun mounting platform with its wicker wrap that prevents the logs from splaying out. A nicely thought-out and executed solution to a problem of a dry firm and level firing platform.

Soldiers are much the same the world over, the gun crew here are posing for a group photo and one of them is clowning around with a practice bomb that they have taken as a souvenir (looted) from the newly occupied French airfield they have recently occupied. Sadly no date other than June 1940 is given and no location information either. Of note however is the bead component of a direct fire ring-and-bead sight that has been fitted to this Flak 30. In the absence of any other gun sight this was the standard back-up installation, the issued *Flakvisier* 35 may have been damaged or lost.

We have here a *Luftwaffe* Flak crew at the ready in a gun pit on the perimeter of an airfield in western Poland during 1941. Note the *Gefreiter* (Lance Corporal) to the right of the gun in the photo, he is seen to be resting a fully loaded spare 20 round magazine on this thigh, a great pose for a diorama.

A nice clean photograph of this Flak 30 on a gunnery range close to the city of Koblenz, Germany, taken in January 1940. Of interest as it offers us not only a good view of the gun but also the eye piece of the EM34 or EM36 *Entfernungsmesser* range finder, being held by second soldier from the left Note: the difference between the EM34 and EM36 *Entfernungsmesser* was only the configuration of the internal lens system; hence the external view of both is exactly the same and both were issued to 2 cm flak crews.

This pair of images is of the same improvised Flak tower on the captured French air airfield of Montdidier, located in northeast France, 90 km NNE of Paris and 2.8 km north of the town of Montdidier. The Flak 30 is mounted atop a wooden platform that has been erected on the observation roof deck of the previous occupant's radio room, using the roof access doorway as a structural support. The photo was taken on 26th August 1940.

This photograph was taken on a parade ground set up in one of the many temporary barracks that appeared outside many German towns during the expansion of Germany's armed forces following the 1933 Nazi takeover of government. Many became prisoner of war camps later after more solid barracks had been constructed for the Germans they were originally intended for. We can see two groups of four Kar 98k Rifles, two 2 cm Flak 30s and an 88 mm Flak 18 set up in line in front of the dais.

Right: An interesting profile photograph of a Flak 30 at its full elevation limit of 90°. It offers us a full view of the elevation radius gear attached to the bottom of the gun cradle and also shows that this is a camouflaged example of the weapon, as witnessed by the change in tonal values on the gear's flat surface.

A very interesting view of a Flak 30 set up to fire whilst still not only attached to its Sd. Ah. 51 transport trailer but also still limbered up to its towing vehicle. Whilst this configuration must have only offered a minimal field of fire, I guess it was a quick way to enable the crew to put up defensive fire if only as a deterrent to protect a convoy it was travelling in.

A nice atmospheric photograph of a Flak 30 set up to defend a roadway next to a canal. The weapon is set up on the canal's raised embankment. The photograph was taken on the very day the Dutch surrendered, 14th May 1940, the location is recorded as being close to the Dutch town of Tiel. The two crew members on top of the embankment are sitting on 2 cm ammunition boxes.

A very clear photograph of this Flak 30 set up on the edge of recently harvested field. Its camouflage paint scheme is most evident as the demarcation of the colours is clearly visible on the gun mount's side panels. The other item rarely seen close up is the top of one of the base levelling pad's winding wheels with its fold down handle, here in the folded down position. Also of note is the clear view of the gun sight and its aim following gear.

On this page we have two more examples of gun emplacements. The top photo shows a Flak 30 on top of a flak tower on the perimeter of the captured French airfield of Montdidier in northeast France that was given the *Luftwaffe* identification code number of 512. The photo was taken on 25th June 1943. The bottom photograph is of a well finished field gun pit installation on the downslope of a hill over-looking the industrial area of Warburg, a small town north-west of Kassel, Germany. Of note is the hole in the wooden clad sides of the pit being used to store ammunition boxes that each contain two twenty-round magazines..

Here we have a photograph that is an exception to the norm, this Flak 30 crew are wearing full battle dress but they are on a range and not in combat. Many things to note here. Firstly the crew are seen in the process of changing a barrel – one man will offer the barrel up to its splined receiver and another will then tighten down the locking collar. The whole change could be done in under 30 seconds in a battle situation. Also note the two spare loaded magazines on the gun's rotating base plate, and the amount of spent cartridge cases on the ground. It is easy to see why a net was used in later weapons to catch these, as in battle conditions they would become a trip hazard for the loader very quickly. Lastly, note the age of this crew – taken in August 1943 we can clearly see proof that by this stage of the war second line units such as stationary point defence weapons were going to be manned by those who, under normal conditions, would have been considered unfit to serve.

Another range photo, this one from July 1942 taken in Meppen, Germany. Of interest amongst this *Luftwaffe* crew is the loader holding a spare magazine ready to reload the Flak 30. It is being held at an angle such that we can see the staggered configuration of the rounds it contains, and the extended lip at its top on one side only to force the rounds into the correct position for the gun's firing block to pick one out as it returns from full recoil having just fired the previous round.

Here we have camouflaged Flak 30 on a firing range in the Hanover area of Germany, photographed on 30th October 1938. Of note here is the late style of gunner's hand wheel – it is flat sided whereas the early Flak 38s were fitted with circular tube-like rimmed hand wheels. Also of note is the gunner pictured in the act of clipping a fully loaded new magazine into the gun's magazine receiver housing.

Photographed in late 1940 somewhere in the Pas de Calais, France, we find this Flak 30 in a neatly finished earthen sided gun pit lined with turf. The crew have placed three wooden boxes into the sides walls of the pit at equally spaced points of the compass as ready ammunition, each holding three ammunition boxes (tins), each of which in turn hold two twenty round magazines. Note that as previously mentioned the individual magazines are placed into the boxes in opposing directions in order to enable them to be picked out of the box easily by hand.

This nicely posed photo was taken by a soldier at an official photo shoot of his unit. No doubt the official photos were more rigidly posed without the gunner smiling for the camera! Of note here is that the gun crew member with the rangefinder is still wearing the metal case for the range finder's shoulder harness on his back.

Below: Here we see another Flak 38 emplaced in an earthen gun pit. This photo however is not a combat photograph as it at seems at first glance, it was taken during a gas attack drill whilst on a field exercise in the summer of 1938. Mostly of note is that this crew are still equipped with the old pre-war GM24 style of gas mask; this type had all but disappeared from frontline military service by beginning of 1940.

Opposite page, top: At the ready, this Flak 30 is photographed somewhere on the central Russia front in the late summer of 1941. The front was moving fast and the best this crew had time to do was to dig a shallow gun pit. Of note is that the crew obviously are aware they might encounter Russian stragglers that were missed by the advancing troops, as their personal weapons are with them close to hand in the gun pit. Note also the EM34 or EM36 *Entfernungsmesser* range finder laid on top of its carrying case in the foreground.

Taken on the 2nd June 1941 on a timber flak tower close to Apeldoorn, Holland, we see a firing drill being undertaken by this Flak 30 crew. Whilst one crewman is loading a full magazine into the gun, another seems to reaching out to do something with the ring of the ring and bead sights. Possibly he is going to turn the ring 90° so it can be of use to the gunner. The ring part of the ring and bead sight could be left attached to the gun whilst any of the other sights were fitted. However in order for it not to obstruct their view it had to be turned out of the way.

Below: Photographed on a cold autumn morning we have here a Flak 30 fitted to its Sd. Ah. 51 transporter trailer that in turn is hitched up to a Krupp Protze L 2 H 43 Kfz. 70 parked outside the control room of a captured French airfield. Sadly all that is recorded about this photo was that it was taken in France during October 1940. Note here the Flak 30 is fitted with its factory-supplied protective canvas cover, easily identified by the loop and toggle fasteners along the join line below the gun's barrel.

Opposite page, top: At last we have here a photo of a Flak 30 fitted with its gun shields. By far the majority of independent Flak 30s (guns not fitted to vehicles as part of a self-propelled weapon system) were not fitted with gun shields. This Flak 30 has been emplaced to protect a bridge in the French city of Rouen. This view of the gun offers us a clear profile of the rear portion of the triangular gun base platform, we can see both the rear levelling foot pad and the base's rear tail skid with the hole in it that was the attachment point for the rear of the gun's base to its Sd. Ah. 51 trailer. Other interesting items on view here are the cobbled road surface around the tram-rails, the steel-framed bridge and in the far right of the photo in the background is a town gas storage tank.

This photo of a cold crew around their Flak 30 in its log built emplacement was taken in December 1941 somewhere close to Vyazma, Russia. Whilst the gun is just a standard 2 cm Flak 30, I am surprised by the apparent youth of two members of the gun crew at this early stage of the war. Had this photograph of a Flak gun crew been taken in 1944 it would not have been uncommon at all. What is common for 1941 however is the total lack of suitable Russian winter clothing.

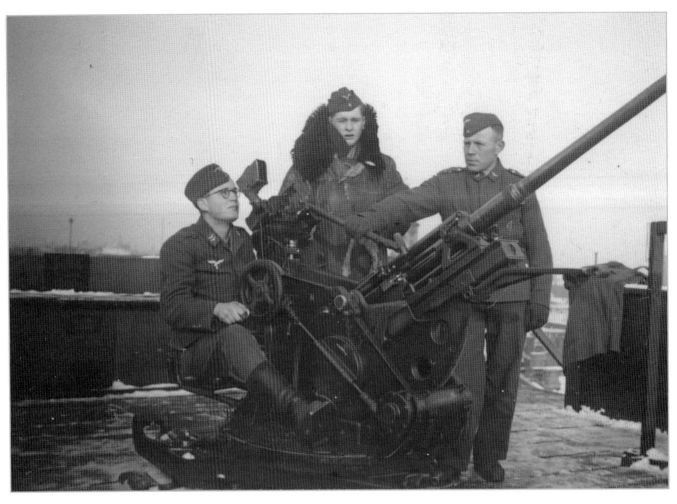

This *Luftwaffe* gun and crew were photographed on a roof top emplacement in the harbour area of Calais, France, on 24th December 1940. At least one member of the crew has managed to acquire a winter coat, that would have been sent from home or acquired privately from a local source, be it purchased or looted.

Below: A battery of 2 cm Flak 30s are seen here on part of the Baltic coast designated as a firing range. Of interest is the pile of equipment in the foreground, amongst which is a carrying case for the shoulder mounting frame for an EM34 or EM36 *Entfernungsmesser* 1 metre range finder – it is the truncated triangular box seen at the very front of the pile with its carrying straps lying on the sand. Behind it is a EM34 or EM36 range finder on top of its stowage box and, lent against it but behind, is the top of an open spare barrel box.

Seen on an elevated log-built firing platform raised above the marshy area it is in is this Flak 30 in overall Panzer Grey. Things to note on this 1942 photograph are the use of the ring and bead sight and the visible word "Braun" stencilled in white paint on the gun cradle recoil housing. It refers to the type of oil to be used in the gun hydraulic recoil system, typically this would be either "Braun" or "Braun-Ark". "Braun-Ark" would usually only be for guns having to operate in very cold conditions (ark=Arctic), in reality crews were forced to use whatever they could get.

Below: This is the same gun and emplacement as in the photo above but is of interest in that it shows the way the weapon's levelling pads have been "chocked" into position by wooden shaped planks fixed to the emplacement floor. Obviously the weapon had a tendency to move under its own recoil forces on a smooth wooden deck, a point that modellers should be aware of.

An action shot of a *Luftwaffe* Flak 30 gun crew getting ready to fire on an incoming target. Whilst this is an action-like pose I am not convinced that it is not posed for effect. Nonetheless it does show a more realist appearance than in the PK (*Propaganda Kompanie*) photos. The shallow earthen gun pit is of interest as we can see ready ammunition boxes that must have been placed on the perimeter of the intended pit and its dug out spoil being stacked up around them. The photo is stated to have been taken on 3rd June 1940 in Belgium.

Below: Seen sat at the edge of the parade ground of Paderborn barracks, Germany, on 17th October 1938, is this pristine 2 cm Flak 30 mounted on its Sd. Ah. 51 transport trailer. This very clear view shows us the tyre tread patterns as well as detail of the way the front of the weapon was picked up by the trailer's hook-like end caps of its "U" shaped tubular frame.

This photo, taken on the bank of the Steinhuder Meer, east of Hanover, Germany, on 5th December 1943, shows us a late version of a fully equipped and updated Flak 30. It has the gun shields and a spent cartridge case catching net. This gun is part of the mobile protection unit that was attached to Wunstorf airfield. Many airfields would have a mobile flak unit attached, so allied reconnaissance could never be entirely sure of where all the flak was going to be located whilst making plans for an attack.

Below: A 2 cm Flak 30 is seen here being set up on a piece of waste ground in the city of Bremen, Germany. It could be as part of an exercise, as Bremen was well protected with prepared positions for flak batteries. The only thing I can state for sure is that the photograph is dated October 1940.

This photo from my collection shows that Flak protection on important targets was updated, as the 2 cm Flak proved to less and less effective due to allied aircraft development. This photo was taken on 13th May 1941 and shows a 2 cm Flak 30 emplacement overlooking a length of the Rhine that was an important supply route for German industry and as such needed to be protected from allied air strikes. I have a photo taken on 4th June 1943 at the same location but the 2 cm Flak 30 has been replaced with a 37 mm Flak 36. Lastly note in this photo the 2 cm ammunition boxes (tins) with the white circular markings on them, both are being used for tools associated with the Flak 30 and have been marked to ensure the crew do not mistake them for ready ammunition when they are in a rush.

Below: A very good photograph of a battery of Dark Brown and Panzer Grey camouflaged 2 cm Flak 30s seen at a firing range outside Magdeburg, Germany, on 22nd May 1939. Their associated towing vehicles are both Krupp Protze L 2 H 143 Kfz. 70s. Notably the crew member with the rangefinder is wearing a leather holster for a P08 Luger automatic pistol and the crew all carry the canvas case for the early GM24 gas mask.

Here we have a gun pit dug into the side of a hill outside the port of le Havre, France, in the summer of 1941. The EM34 or EM36 *Entfernungsmesser* 1 metre rangefinder mounted on a tripod is of note as is the relaxed attitude to uniform code. "What the officers don't see will not hurt us" is a common attitude throughout the world's military. Also of interest is the apple orchard the emplacement is next to – these apples are at the core of the Calvados cider that takes its name from this department of France.

Below: This Flak 30 crew are seen posing for a group photo whilst gathered around their gun that is located on top of what looks to be a very sturdily built timber flak tower on the outskirts of Dulmen, Germany, south-west of the city of Munster. Note the flimsy looking timber hand rails mounted on the wooden floor of the flak tower. They are in fact not hand rails at all, it is a crude frame that was erected to prevent the gunner depressing the gun low enough to fire directly into the industrial site they are defending whilst he was fully engaged in tracking a possible low flying enemy aircraft making a strafing attack on the target.

A nice profile shot of a gun crew ready for action, it looks as though it could have been taken almost anywhere on the Western Front. In fact other than the recorded date on the reverse of the photo stating it was taken in August 1937, and the Pre-War style of gas masks they are wearing, it would have been hard to tell.

On a misty morning this Flak 30 is being given a wipe down by two of its crew members to get rid of the condensation formed on the weapon. The photograph is dated March 1940 and was taken in the Koblenz area, I assume, as other photos in the album this comes from were all taken there. The difference between the two crews member's uniform colours is striking. The issued overalls (fatigue uniform known as Drillichanzug) that were commonly worn during training or for work details such as cleaning weapons, as seen here, were made of undyed linen or cotton until the beginning of 1940 when they were issued dyed green. In this photo we can see one of each.

On this page we have two photographs of the same 2 cm Flak 30 that has been emplaced on a railway wagon with low sidewalls. The gun is fixed to the wooden floor. The crew can be seen in various relaxed poses, in the top photograph one crew member is smoking whilst another is seen rolling a cigarette of his own, in the bottom photo we can see a card game in progress, and one crew member reading a newspaper. In both photos ammunition boxes are being used as seats and we even have a milk churn in sight in the top photo as well. This type of improvised flak wagon was a common sight throughout the war on all fronts, and even in most occupied territories due to local resistance activities. Pas de Calais August 1940. (Both photos B. Belcarz)

An atmospheric photograph of a 2 cm Flak 30 gun position in a reed bed and as that is all that was to hand, that is what the crew have used to line the gun pit with (field craft 101). Sadly I have no information as to date and location, but as the crew are *Luftwaffe* it might be part of an airfield perimeter guard, but that's just a guess. (B. Belcarz)

Below: "The happy little band at work" – a great photo to be sent home, seen in their gun pit manning their 2 cm Flak 30 this crew offer a most comfortable pose. The photograph was taken at Sint-Jan-op-den-Dijk in Belgium, just south of the port of Zeebrugge. This gun pit dug into a field with a slight incline offers us yet another view of field craft – here we see a tarpaulin used to line the back walls and the log and plank retainer at the lower front edge that also doubles as a drain for rain water to gather in, rather than the pit floor. Also note the use of the ubiquitous sand bags to bulk up the surrounding bund. The photo is dated 2nd June 1940, whilst the battle of Dunkirk rages only few miles further down the coast.

Another 2 cm Flak 30 atop a Flak tower, built on the roof of the factory that the weapon is tasked to protect, here the Marienfelde plant where Mercedes manufactured the L3000 3 ton truck as well as various aero engines. This very clear view gives us a look at much of the detail around the sighting system, and clearly shows us the follower mechanism that keeps the sights focused on the same spot as the gun is pointed at. Also of note is the ranging profile aid pinned on to the surrounding emplacement wall, a church spire is drawn in silhouette with its range noted in the top right corner of the drawing.

A snow-covered parade ground in Leipzig, Germany, where the photograph was taken on 12th February 1939. In view we have two Flak 30s, both of which are loaded up in their Sd. Ah. 51 trailers that have the rear support leg extended that served to both level the gun whilst still mounted in the trailer and enabled it to be fired from that position in an emergency. However as the leaf spring suspension of the two wheels that provided the other points of ground contact could not be locked up, the gun would have bounced around and been very inaccurate – but would have still provided a deterrent to any attacking low level aircraft.

This photo of a *Luftwaffe* light Flak unit shows them learning how to hit ground targets as they undertake a live firing exercise on Lüneburg Heath, Germany. However the most dominant part of the image is the senior NCO (non-commissioned officer) looking through his binoculars in the centre of the photograph.

A light mobile Flak unit seen setting up a 2 cm Flak 30 in a temporary location somewhere on or around the *Luftwaffe* airbase at Lannion, in western France in the French department of Brittany, given the code number 330. Lannion was expanded a lot by the Germans and by 1943 it had transformed from a simple grass airfield in 1940 to a main base with a concrete runway and many hangers, some of which can be seen in the background of this photo. The crew are pictured uncoupling the rear of weapon's base plate from its Sd. Ah. 51 trailer.

Yet another very well built and established flak emplacement built for this Flak 30 in the Hook of Holland. seen in June 1942. By 1944 this location was part of a concrete bunker complex that was part of the Atlantic Wall, however here we see the original timber-sided gun pit with built-in ready ammunition storage positions and outside the bund just visible is a bicycle, no doubt commandeered by the crew for trips to-and-fro. Lastly in the background we can see the timber and turf covered crew living quarters.

Both the photographs on this page show a Flak 30 mounted on a firing platform built on the roof of an office block in the city centre of Bielefeld, Germany. Many such roof-top installations were constructed from 1942 onwards, they were a very effective method of giving flak guns an unobstructed field of vision and fire, but often the type and size of gun was dictated by the structural integrity of the roof concerned. According to the notation in the album these came from, the *Luftwaffe* soldiers in the photo are not the actual crew but a bunch of other (good looking) soldiers brought in for an official photo PK photo taken later.

Top: Here we have a gun pit overlooking the Pivdennyl Buh River south of Voznesensk, in the Ukraine, photographed on 27th August 1941. The Flak 30 is seen with both its ring-and-bead sight, albeit not set up, and its 3x8 telescopic sights fitted for engaging ground targets.

Right: This Flak 30 is one of the few fitted with its gun shields, although the middle part of the shield that the gun barrel protruded through is missing. This was not uncommon as often the need to change a barrel quickly outweighed the little extra protection that small part of the three part gun shield offered, as it had to be removed before the crew could get access to the barrel's locking nut/ferrule. This photo is of one *Unteroffizier* Paul Ritterman, the gunner, wearing his fatigue uniform (*Drillichanzug*), taken to send home to his wife Berta. I had the pleasure of working with their son in the 1990s and it was he who gave me this photo. Photo dated July 1942, no location given but he served somewhere on the Eastern Front.

A field demonstration of the setting up of a Flak 30 so that it is ready to fire whilst still attached to its Sd. Ah. 51 trailer. The operation of this Flak 30 is being watched by senior *Luftwaffe* officers on 4th June 1938, during an exercise on the military training grounds outside the city of Munster, Germany.

This photo comes from the invasion of the Low Countries in May 1940 and shows a Flak 30 set up in a field close to one of the advanced airstrips temporarily used by the *Luftwaffe* in order to be able to deliver close support to the German fast moving front line troops. The date written on the photos reverse is 30th May 1940 but unfortunately no location is given. Note the use of a standard issue German World War One vintage tent.

Taken in Frankfurt, Germany, in March of 1936 we have a Flak 30 being used to train future weapons instructors. This is the earliest photo I have of the type, although it entered service with the *Luftwaffe* in late 1934. This site that we can see here with its wooden accommodation buildings was totally changed when they built a large brick three storey barrack complex on this site, starting construction in September of the same year.

Bottom: This photo taken close to Bad Tolz, Germany, on a fresh summer morning in 1937 was just one engagement undertaken by this display unit that year. The German military had many display teams that toured the whole country, to both encourage enlistment but also to lend credence to the Nazi doctrine that the Army is the People and the People are the Army, that all Germany was one co-operative unit working for a greater Germany. Sadly it worked.

Here we have a Flak 30 emplaced in a meadow in western Belgium seen on 29th May 1940, note the amount of ready ammunition to hand that bears testimony to the activity the RAF was undertaking in the area in a protective role over the Dunkirk beaches. The RAF was much maligned by the troops rescued from Dunkirk but in fact they put up a furious fight inland to deter and even turn back many bombing raids on route to the beaches. Also of note is the crew tent made from buttoned together ponchos with helmets used to cover tent pole holes, also the Sd.Kfz. 251 armoured half-track parked in the background that may indicate that the Flak gun is to here protect a troop position on the Dunkirk perimeter.

Left: This Flak 30 crew and their weapon are undergoing an inspection. The officer is pointing out a fault, no doubt, as they do on inspections to justify their existence (as soldiers everywhere would believe). This picture was taken at the Paderborn training grounds in Germany during March 1938.

Right: This is a very odd emplacement, the concrete pedestals the Flak 30 is placed upon are proof this was not a temporary installation yet the gun remains totally exposed out in the open with no protective surround of any type. All I can tell from the photo's inscription is that it was taken in June 1941, on the Baltic coast somewhere called Rewa, although the writing is smudged. Possibly Riga or Rewal?

A Flak 30 seen on top of a timber built Flak tower in the Oberhausen area of Germany. Many such timber flak towers in this important industrial area of Germany were replaced with purpose-built concrete flak towers as the war progressed. This Flak 30 was photographed on 27th May 1941 at the "Rangierbahnhof Oberhausen Osterfeld" which looking at other photos from this sequence seems to have been a major railway rolling stock marshalling yard.

A great photo of a gunner at the ready and on lookout, the general worn appearance and the look of intense concentration on his face brings me to believe this is not a posed photo but one that shows the strain of battle. The soldier in the background appears to building up the turf sod wall to help both conceal and protect the gun emplacement. All I have on this photo is that it was taken in June 1940 but I have no other info sadly.

Here we see a Flak 30 emplaced in a shallow gun pit on the perimeter of an airfield recently captured during the headlong advance into France following the defeat of the western allies in the north. Note the loader is just about to clip on a fully loaded magazine into the gun, also the ring and bead sights are fitted in the absence of the a *Flakvisier* 35 gun sight. This photo is dated 19ᵗʰ June 1940 again I have no location information on the photo other than that it was taken at a French airfield

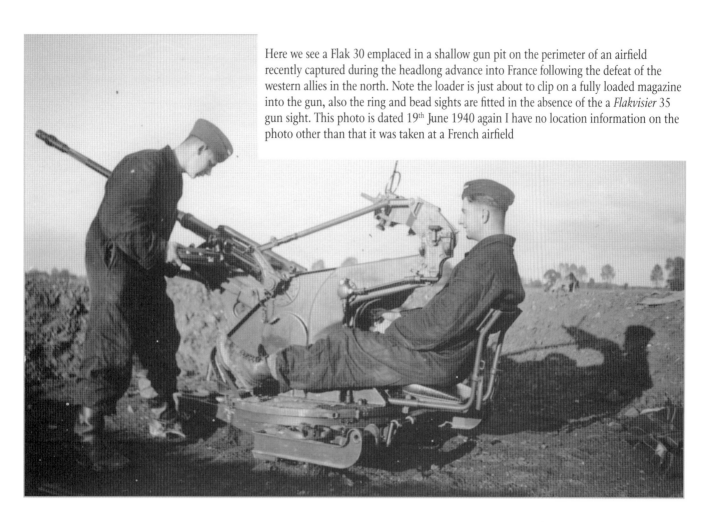

This quality photograph of a light anti-aircraft unit at home in their barracks in Munich, Germany, was taken in August 1937. Note the small mud flaps on the mudguards of the Sd. Ah. 51 trailers, not a common detail to be able to made out with any clarity. Also the tread pattern on the tyres is seen clearly. Lastly the travel locks on both the guns in view are unlocked and the locking bars are seen in their raised position under the gun cradle.

This clear close-up of the profile of a *Luftwaffe* flak gunner also gives us a fantastic look at the *Flakvisier* 35 gunsight and its mounting location on the 2 cm Flak 30. Of note here is the *Flakvisier* 35 gunsight's electric cable that is unplugged and coiled around the sight's mounting point. The *Flakvisier* 35 needed power to light the bulb that illuminated the graticule (The reticle graduated pattern in an optical instrument). Sliding glass plates within the gunsight could be adjusted to give the gunner the correct aiming point. Note also the black leather cover sewn around the outer rim of the gunner's elevation control hand wheel.

This is a great photo of a 2 cm Flak 30 and s crew set up in a Brussels street during the early days of the invasion. Flak guns are rarely seen set up in city streets as the surrounding buildings drastically reduce both visibility and indeed field of fire when the gun is at ground level. Whilst it is not stated, the weapon is probably part of a point defence system that was emplaced around a strategically important location. I know Brussels quite well but do not recognise the location, however many such buildings are in evidence just outside the city centre area. I can only assume the weapon was placed to provide protection to a command unit's billet during the invasion, as the photo was taken on 27th May 1940, the day before the Belgium surrender. Lastly of note in this photograph is the clear detail of the rarely fitted gun shield.

A well dug-in 2 cm Flak 30 emplacement with a high mud and turf surrounding bund. Within this protective structure the Flak 30, fitted with its armoured gun shield, is ready for action. In the foreground we can see a stowage box that contains an EM34 or EM36 *Entfernungsmesser* 1 metre range finder. A tripod for it has been put up next to it. On the top of the bund on the left of the photo is a closed spare 2 cm barrel box that contained two spare barrels and associated tools, as well as a cleaning rod broken down into three screw together sections. This photo was taken in May 1942 in Orsha, now a city in Belarus. The weapon is located close to an important railway line.

A pre-war photo of a Flak 30 emplaced in the open somewhere on the training grounds used by troops based in Koblenz, Germany. This photo is one of a series of photos taken by an accomplished photographer. However, sadly for me, over 80% of his excellent photos are of locations and individuals at play, at rest or eating, not the equipment that this publication is focused upon.

Taken within the confines of the barracks in Nuremburg, Germany, this photo shows a ceremony where six senior NCOs are swearing the "Fuhrer Oath" on 12th September 1934. The "Führer Oath" had been in use since 2nd August 1934, but did not become mandatory by law until July 1935. Seen in front of the dais are two Flak 30s and two pyramids of four Kar 98ks each.

This informal Flak crew photograph was taken around a 2 cm Flak 30 emplaced on a roof top flak platform built on the multi-storey office block of Demag's Duisburg Factory, next to an inland harbour on the River Rhine. It was taken on 17th April 1942.

Emplaced on the reverse slopes of sand dunes on the Pas de Calais, somewhere close to the French village of Wissant where its crew were billeted, this Flak 30 is barely dug in at all. But in a short time (only weeks) this gun and crew had moved into cleaned-out, repaired and upgraded French built concrete emplacements. This set of emplacements were extended again to become one of the most fortified areas within the Atlantic Wall defence system. Note in the background the open spare barrel box, whilst the spare barrels cannot be seen as they are in the bottom half of the box. We can see the three part cleaning rod in its stowed position.

This Flak 30 is actually mounted onto a railway flatbed wagon but that cannot be seen from this angle. Other shots from the same source are so badly focused as to be unusable, sadly. However what can be seen of interest in this photo is that the gunner, whilst being well wrapped up in his greatcoat, is also sitting on what looks to be a folded up blanket, to try and make the gunner's seat more comfortable on the long journey ahead.

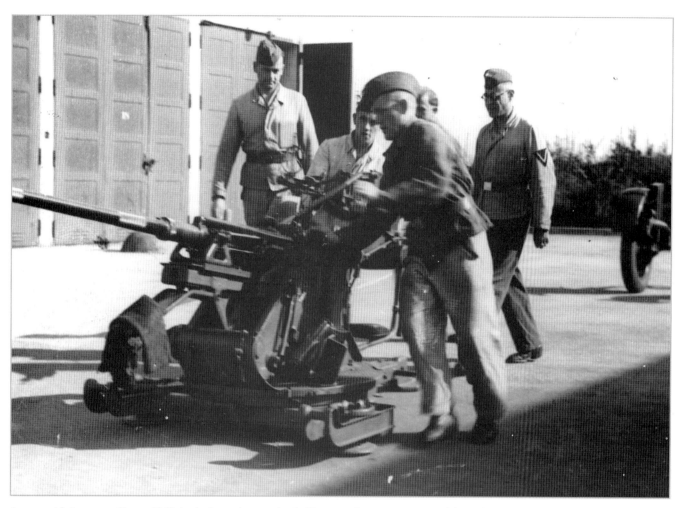

Seen outside its garage (Panzer Hall) in the barracks complex in Hanover, Germany, we see a Flak 30 that is about to undergo a good cleaning. The photo was taken on 16th May 1938.

This Flak 30 sits at the ready in a gun pit that is slightly odd in that it is a pit that has been dug down about a foot, and then an a circular trench has been dug around the base area of a Flak 30 to produce a lower working area for the gun crew. This trench has made a pedestal for the gun to be mounted upon that has had a wooden wall built to support its sides. The odd part is, where has all the soil gone? Normally it would have been used to make a bund around the position but here there is none.

A scene common to all wars and armies, the "hurry up and wait". This gun crew is on watch at the ready to protect the factory complex seen in the background and the railway next to it. However the gunner is writing something and the loader is reading a book, such was the boredom of most days, action when it came would be fast and hectic. This photo was taken close to the town of Frankenthal, Germany, in July 1942.

Taken in Libya this photograph shows a Horch Kfz. 69, the prime mover for this 2 cm Flak 30 anti-aircraft gun seen in the foreground. The crew are in the process of unhitching the 2 cm Flak from its Sd. Ah. 51 trailer. Note the extra-long protective sleeve fitted in an effort to prevent the all-pervasive fine sand from getting into the barrel.

The two photographs on this page show the same 2 cm Flak 30 in the summer of 1939. These laid back *Luftwaffe* troops are seen posing around their weapon on this hot sunny day, just outside the perimeter fence of the Heinkel North Plant in Rostock-Marienehe, now known as Rostock-Schmarl on the west bank of the Unterwarnow estuary. The Flak 30 is fitted with its ring and bead sights only, both the 3x8 telescopic sight for engaging ground targets and its *Flakvisier* 35 electronic gun sight are absent. Of note is the very clear contrast between the two-tone Panzer Grey and Dark Green camouflage paint scheme.

A 2 cm Flak 30 stands guard over the coal mine outside the town of La Houve in France, a mine that is only 10 km from the Luxembourg border and 20 km from both Belgium and Germany. The flak crew are posing whilst on watch and are at the ready. Of interest is the observer standing to the left of the photo wearing the shoulder steadying harness for the EM34 or EM36 *Entfernungsmesser* 1 metre range finder that he is holding down by his side. The weapon is set up just off a typical French tree-lined road with the mine's slagheap in the background. Taken in January of 1941. (B. Belcarz)

This Flak 30 with a full set of armoured gun shields is set up to protect the river crossings we see in the background. A good selection of field engineered bridging is in evidence, the original railway bridge in the background that has been repaired and reinforcement added to its wooden pylons, a German army engineers prefabricated bridge in the middle and closest to the camera a log and pontoon improvised bridge that no doubt was constructed first during the advance. The location is given as north of Ternopil, in the Ukraine, so the river is probably the Seret. Lastly note the crew's pet/mascot, a dog. Many crews would adopt a pet on their travels.

A Flak 30 in a shallow gun pit is set up outside the perimeter of Carpiquet airfield close to the village of Rots where the crew were billeted. The photo was taken on 2nd October 1940. The soldier on guard has been photographed by his friend whilst having dropped off to sleep. Of interest is the practice bomb that has been used as a joke sticking out of the small spoil pile in front of the gun pit.

Right: This 2 cm Flak 30 has been set up on the buttress of a destroyed bridge over the river Meuse that is undergoing temporary field repairs. Whilst the engineers are hard at work below, the gun crew have made themselves comfortable by commandeering chairs from a house close by. This photo was taken on 16th May, just after the battle for Sedan that was just to the north of this bridge.

This overexposed photograph was taken during a light-hearted moment on the cliffs above Le Havre, France, on the occasion of the gunner Hans Max's 21st birthday. Sadly the actual date is not recorded on the photo but the summer of 1941 is stated on other photos from this group.

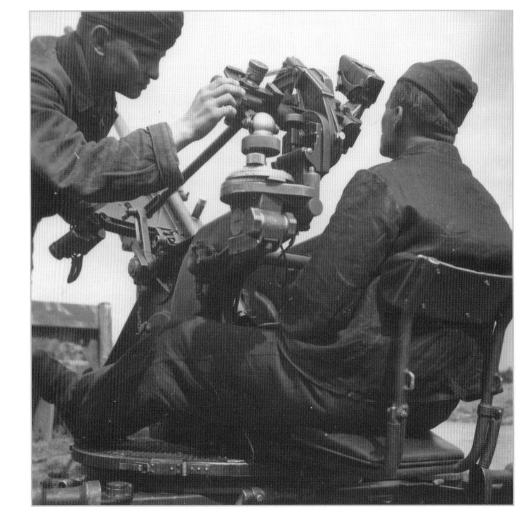

Right: Here we see the sighting mechanism being adjusted on a Flak 30, the crewman looks to be adjusting the gun sight's follower arm setting. This good overall view of the sighting mechanism was taken on a *Luftwaffe* firing range on the Baltic coast in August 1939.

A soldier is pictured here posing on the gunner's seat of this Flak 30, set up whilst still attached to its Sd. Ah. 51 trailer. The weapon is not set up to fire however as the travel lock under the recoil system (gun cradle) is still locked to the trailer's body. The trailer has its levelling leg deployed so the gun could, if unlocked, fire from this position. Also note the bracket for the sights is also folded down in its travel position.

Below: This Flak 30 is emplaced in a flak tower in Bremerhaven, Germany. It's mounted on a naval pedestal mount, many of both this type and other naval mounts found their way into land locked installations as the ship building program of the German Navy was slashed on Hitler's orders, after he became disenchanted with the surface fleet following several high value losses. The stock of weapon systems that were already manufactured to be placed on board ships was reassigned to point defence duties all over the Reich.

Here we have a Flak 30 mounted on a Demag D7 Halftrack to form the mobile antiaircraft vehicle known as an Sd.Kfz 10/4. This is a very early production version of that weapon system and it is seen here at the ready guarding a river crossing over the Moselle River in north-eastern France during the early stages of the invasion of May 1940. Note the non-standard larger box fitted to the Sd.Anh. 51 trailer and the crew's personal equipment scattered all over the firing platform. This photo would make an excellent guide/template for an interesting and busy little diorama.

Right: Note for more detail and much more photographic information on the Flak 30 mounted on the Sd.Kfz. 10/4 please refer to Camera On No. 8, titled Sd.Kfz. 10/4 & 10/5 *Selbstfahrlafette*. Just one of the many books in the series on German WWII soft skin vehicles.

ALAN RANGER

MMPBOOKS

SD.KFZ. 10/4 & 10/5
SELBSTFAHRLAFETTE

CAMERA ON ————— 8